# 60 WAYS TO FEEL AMAZING

## Lynda Field

D1164276

# E L E M E N T

**Shaftesbury, Dorset • Boston, Massachusetts**

**Melbourne, Victoria**

© Element Books 1998

Text © Lynda Field 1998

First published in Great Britain in 1998 by
Element Books Limited
Shaftesbury, Dorset SP7 8BP

Published in the USA in 1998 by
Element Books, Inc.
160 North Washington Street, Boston MA 02114

Published in Australia in 1998 by
Element Books
and distributed by Penguin Australia Limited
487 Maroondah Highway, Ringwood, Victoria 3134

Reprinted August, October and December 1998
Reprinted 1999

Cover design by Mark Slader
Design and Typesetting by Drum Enterprises Limited
Printed and bound by Bemrose Security Printing, Derby

British Library Cataloguing in Publication
data available

Library of Congress Cataloging in Publication
data available

ISBN 1 86204 352 3

Dedicated to my youngest son, Alex Field,
who *is* amazing

# INTRODUCTION

*Life is a precious gift, miraculous and amazing but we are not always able to appreciate this miracle fully. When we face obstacles and difficulties our lives can become such a struggle that we lose touch with the amazingness of it all. This little book is full of ways to bring back the magic into your life. All the techniques are simple, practical and tried and tested many times. Use this book to help you to feel as amazing as you truly are.*

Lynda Field

# GO BOLDLY

What is worrying you? What are you afraid of? What is standing in your way?

Our biggest fear is of fear itself and the greatest antidote to fear is boldness.

Boldness releases powerful forces into the universe.

Whenever we act boldly, and give it all we've got, our bodies go into a state of emergency and unlock many underused powers that we all possess, including energy, creativity, strength, stamina, endurance, flexibility and commitment.

☼ *Face Your Fear.*

☼ *Think Boldly.*

☼ *Act Boldly.*

☼ *Feel Amazing.*

# CREATE PEACE
# OF MIND

*Memorize peacefulness*
The next time you see a beautiful
peaceful scene, close your eyes and
commit the view to memory. Make a
collection of peaceful scenes and
memories and replay them whenever
you feel the need. Let the pictures
cross your mind. They will act like a
healing balm.

☆ *Act instead of reacting*
   Peace comes when we take charge of
   our lives. When a problem comes
   along don't be a victim who just
   reacts, face the problem assertively
   and *act*.

Try this two-fold approach to achieve peace
of mind and to realize your true potential.

# BE AN ENCOURAGER

Who do you know who could do with some encouragement right now?

Maybe it's you. One of the surest ways to give yourself hope is to inspire someone else.

People have good intentions, they want to communicate and they want to be creative.

These qualities may not always be obvious but be assured that they are always there (however deeply buried).

So how can you be an encourager?

Think of someone who encouraged you. What did they say? What did they do?

Do the same for someone else. When you start to inspire another person you will feel inspired yourself.

# Bring Your Skeletons
# Out of the Closet

Everyone has thought and done things that they wished they hadn't.

We all make mistakes. But if you have hidden these things away you are also carrying a burden of guilt and shame, as well as the fear that they will be revealed.

Open the closet and bring out your skeletons.

☆ *Invite them out for an airing.*

☆ *Survey each one coolly.*

☆ *Remedy anything that you can.*

☆ *Let them rattle off in peace.*

Your energy will increase and you will feel amazing.

# STOP COMPARISON SHOPPING

When we are feeling low we often compare ourselves unfavourably with others.

We go 'comparison shopping' where we 'buy into' the concept of a comparative scale of self worth: *I'm not as beautiful as … but I'm more beautiful than … or I'm not clever enough/good enough to do that.*

Do you ever compare yourself with others?

Next time you start to compare yourself with someone else become aware of what you are doing and stop!

Say instead, *I am good enough*. You are a unique person. Make positive affirmations about yourself and your life will become a positive experience.

# GIVE YOUR
# BACK A REST

Try this exercise:

- ☆ Lie down on your back, upper arms resting on the floor and hands resting on your abdomen.

-☆- Support your head with a small cushion so that your head is in line with the rest of your body.

-☆- Pull up your legs, knees pointing to the ceiling. Keep your knees apart and your feet flat on the floor. Feel how this brings your lower back closer to the floor.

Rest like this for just a few minutes every day and feel the difference in your energy levels.

# IMPROVE YOUR SEX LIFE

Try the following:

- Focus your attention on your sex life. If it's losing its appeal talk about it, *to each other*.

- Put the romance back into your relationship. Remember what turned you on in the first place.

☆ Spend time alone with each other, turn off the television and enjoy each other.

☆ Laugh together. A great sense of humour is a terrific turn on!

☆ Break some of your comfortable/boring routines. You will know what these are!

# TOUCH YOUR SOUL

Soul food cannot be bought at the supermarket. If the words 'spiritual' and 'soul' mean very little to you, think about a time when you felt 'touched' by something greater than yourself.

Let's touch that shining essence again.

☆ Close your eyes and relax.

☆ Put your right hand over your heart and say to yourself 'I breathe the soul's breath'.

☆ Exhale and wait until your breath naturally comes to you to fill the space.

☆ When your breath *comes to you* in this way you are breathing the soul's breath.

When you do this exercise you will feel fabulous!

# ACCEPT A COMPLIMENT

Why do we find it so hard to accept a compliment gracefully?

How do you feel when someone pays you a compliment? Perhaps you don't believe them. Do you make throwaway comments that spoil the effect of the compliment?

How do you feel if you compliment someone and they don't accept it? Would you bother to do it again?

Learn to accept a compliment. The next time someone says something nice about you just say 'thank you'. It might be difficult but keep on trying.

Accept a compliment and you will feel wonderful and so will the person giving it.

# FINISH AN UNCOMPLETED JOB

How many of your creative inspirations are lying unfinished in the cupboard?

We all have half-completed jobs that we don't finish but which we continually think we *ought* to finish.

These unfinished projects are wind-ups –
throw them out and forget about them forever
*or* finish them.

☆ *Make a list of all your unfinished jobs.*

☆ *Decide which ones can hit the rubbish bin.*

☆ *Choose one of the rest and FINISH IT!*

Your self-respect will reach dizzy heights.

# CELEBRATE YOUR ALONENESS

You are unique.

There is no such thing as a normal or average size or type of person. Everyone is absolutely special and individual.

When we recognize our uniqueness we also recognize our aloneness.

Repeat the following affirmation which will help you to accept and enjoy the inevitability of feeling alone:

*I am sitting on top of the world and I belong to nobody and nobody belongs to me.*

As you say this affirmation use your imagination and visualize yourself at the top of the world feeling wonderful and free.

# RE-INVENT YOURSELF

Do something which is out of character.
Here are a few ideas.

☆ Change your style of dress.

☆ How long have you had the same
hairstyle? More than a year? Change it.

☆ Find a new friend, someone who is quite unlike you.

☆ Start a new hobby or join a nightclass.

☆ Change your make-up/aftershave.

☆ Do you always wear dark colours? Put on some bright clothes and feel the difference.

☆ Visit a different restaurant.

☆ Go to a different pub.

Change is like a breath of fresh air, enjoy the new perspectives it brings.

# USE YOUR ANGER

We are often afraid of our anger, it is a powerful force. So, when the sparks are about to fly we can become confused by a mixture of emotions, including resentment, hatred, guilt and fear.

The next time this happens try the following four steps.

☀ Accept your anger and allow yourself to *feel* it.

☀ Recognize that this is your own powerful energy.

☀ Visualize a volcano going off inside you, filling you with power and energy.

☀ This initial inner blast will clear your mind so that you can act and speak coherently and assertively.

Learn to use your anger constructively.

# Take a Shower
## of Light

Whenever you need a lift, whether it is to energize yourself or to 'throw light' on a problem, try taking a shower of light.

Imagine that you are standing under a shower. See large drops of white light falling over you and enveloping you.

Feel the light as it embraces you. See the white light turn into the colours of the rainbow. Feel and absorb the colours. When you are ready, mentally turn off the shower.

Put your co-workers in a shower of white light and see the difference in your working day!

# Consciously Change Your Environment Everyday

Research shows that the more we feel able to express ourselves positively in our environment the more relaxed and happy we are able to become.

Every day do something to make your surroundings more beautiful.

EXAMPLES

- ☆ Put fresh flowers in your bedroom.
- ☆ Bring a photo for your desk at work.
- ☆ Change a room around.
- ☆ Wash the curtains.
- ☆ Put a plant in your office.
- ☆ Move the pictures around in your house.
- ☆ Play beautiful music while you do the housework.
- ☆ Light a candle when you sit down for a meal.

Give your surroundings some Tender Loving Care and feel the difference.

# PRAISE A CHILD

When we recognize children in a positive way we are helping them to develop good, positive emotional and behaviour patterns: we are developing their self-esteem.

Using praise is one of the most powerful ways of allowing a child to feel good about herself.

There is nothing quite like the feeling you get when you encourage a child to feel good about herself – everyone gets a warm glow!

If you haven't got a child go out and find one to appreciate! Praise a niece, a nephew, a next door neighbour – they will feel great and so will you.

# LAUGH YOURSELF SILLY

How do you feel when you have had a really good laugh? You feel great, don't you?

Laughing and smiling actually have amazing health-giving effects.

Laughter really *is* the best medicine.

You can't have a really good laugh and be anxious at the same time. Begin with a smile, a smile can start to change your mood.

Seek out something that has made you laugh in the past – a video, a book, the company of a certain friend, an activity … Put a smile on your face and go for laughter.

It can only make you feel 100 per cent better.

# CLEAN YOUR AURA

Sit comfortably, close your eyes, steady your breathing and relax.

Be aware of the energy surrounding you: this is your aura. Imagine a halo of light around your entire body; visualize an unbroken line of light encircling you.

Now send a white beam of cleansing light around the contour of your aura.

Imagine this light as a vacuum cleaner sucking out any dirt or negativity. When your aura looks bright and clean open your eyes.

With your freshly cleansed aura you will feel like a million dollars. Clean your aura regularly to maintain good health and positive energy.

# ACHIEVE YOUR GOALS

Someone once said that if you get in a car and don't know where you are going you will never get there.

If we have no goal how can we ever achieve anything?

The successful completion of short-term goals leads inevitably to the achievement of long-term goals as we gain confidence in our ability to make things happen.

☆ Specify three short-term goals.

☆ Make your goals real: write them down.

☆ Give yourself a time limit. (Deadlines can be great motivators.)

☆ Reward yourself with a real prize when you reach your goal.

You will feel brilliant.

# FORGIVE YOUR PARENTS

Remember, your parents did the best they could.

We can only teach and pass on what we already know, and that is what they did.

You may have recognized some of your own negative behaviours, thoughts and feelings in your parents.

You cannot let go of negativity and replace it with positivity if you are still blaming your parents.

Let go of whatever you think your parents 'did' to you. Start to forgive your parents and you will start to feel like a new person.

Remember, your parents had parents too!

# REFRAME YOUR SITUATION

This might be hard to believe, but nothing is actually stressful in itself.

Stress lies in the eye of the beholder. In other words, if you see a person, situation or event as threatening you will register stress.

☆ Think of a personal situation which is a problem for you right now.

☆ Visualize the problem in glorious technicolor. Now, drain all the colour out of the picture.

☆ Shrink the picture until it disappears.

☆ Replace it with a bright, new, positive image in which all your problems have been resolved.

Reframe your negative pictures to take the stress out of your life.

# RECEIVE AN
# ANGELIC BLESSING

Transfer the words below on to paper or
card, to make your own set of Angelic
Blessing Cards.

These cards provide key words that will help
you to focus on particular aspects of your
inner life.

| | | |
|---|---|---|
| SIMPLICITY | ENTHUSIASM | HEALING |
| SPONTANEITY | INSPIRATION | HONESTY |
| HUMOUR | COURAGE | TRUTH |
| BEAUTY | HARMONY | CREATIVITY |
| COMPASSION | FORGIVENESS | TENDERNESS |
| FAITH | UNDERSTANDING | FREEDOM |
| LOVE | INTEGRITY | BALANCE |

Lay out your cards face downwards in front of you. Focus on a problem and ask for divine assistance. Choose a card and reflect on its meaning. Absorb the qualities that this blessing brings.

Strengthen your divine connection and amazing things will start to happen.

# BELIEVE THAT YOU DESERVE THE BEST

If you don't believe that you deserve the best then you will not allow good things into your life.

 Do you think that you deserve to fulfil your dreams?

☀ Do you deserve the best that life has to offer?

☀ Do you believe that you don't deserve very much or, in fact, that you deserve nothing at all?

Closely examine your beliefs about what you think you deserve. Repeat this affirmation over and over:

*I deserve the best in life.*

Say it in the car, sing it in the shower. Believe that you deserve the best and you will get it!

# Accentuate the Positive, Eliminate the Negative

Thoughts are powerful things; whatever you put your attention to will grow.

Think negatively and your life will spiral into depression.

Replace negatives with positives.

☼ If you feel angry think the biggest loving thought that you can. There's not room for both thoughts.

☼ If you feel rushed, stop, close your eyes and visualize a beautiful calm scene.

☼ If you feel like a loser repeat the affirmation *'I am a winner'*.

When we can fill our minds with beautiful thoughts our world becomes a beautiful place.

# REMEMBER BE HERE NOW

If you get so organized and together that you are busy living in the future *or* you are rushing to keep track of time, then you are missing the true pleasure of the moment.

Whenever you feel that your life is running out of control, stop and say to yourself:

*'Remember, be here now!'*

The power is always in the moment. Stop reading and recognize the moment, *feel the now.*

'Later' never actually exists because we are only ever really conscious in the present moment and 'later' always lies in the future.

Appreciate this precious moment of your life.

# IDENTIFY AND ELIMINATE UNNECESSARY STRESSORS

A certain amount of stress encourages us to achieve and to be dynamic in our lives as we learn to overcome life's challenges.

However, too much stress can cause exhaustion, depression, lethargy and even illness.

We all react differently to situations. One person's stress exhilarator ('Yes, I *can* meet that deadline') is another person's stress poison ('it's all too much for me').

Identify and list the unnecessary stress in your life. Think carefully about each stressor. How can you let go of it, change it or accept it?

Change your approach and release harmful stress.

# SPICE UP
# YOUR LIFE

Here is a fantastic technique which is
practical and mind-expanding at the same
time.

You can do it anywhere and create an
amazing experience for yourself.

It's called 'self-remembering' and introduces the concept of the 'witness'.

The witness observes all your doings but does not judge your actions in any way.

If it feels hard to observe yourself in this way just imagine that you are standing outside of your body watching yourself. (Don't spend time analysing this method, just do it!)

Take your witness to the supermarket and have an ecstatic shopping experience!

# USE YOUR TIME HAPPILY

Are you managing your time efficiently and happily? Are you able to make time for the things you love to do?

List the way your time is used in different activities throughout the week.

☆ Now list those activities that give you the most fulfilment.

☆ Compare your lists.

What are the differences between the two? How could you manage your time to allow for more personal satisfaction?

Learn to make the very best use of your time; it is your most valuable resource.

# REPLACE 'SHOULD' WITH 'COULD'

Write down all the things that you think that you should do:

I should:..............................................................

Now, take each 'I should' from your list, read it out loud and then ask yourself, 'Why should I?'

Rewrite your list, replacing 'should' with 'could' and start each statement with, 'If I really wanted to'.

Rewrite your list in this way and you might find that there are some things that you don't even want to change!

Don't be a 'should' victim, trapped by guilt. Allow yourself the possibility of 'could' and you will become free to allow positive changes into your life.

# MAKE A
# SUCCESS LIST

When we are feeling low in self-esteem it is difficult to like anything about ourselves.

When we are caught in a negative spiral of: self-dislike ➜ feelings of powerlessness ➜ inability to make decisions ➜ inability to act ➜ self-dislike.

There is a way to stop the rot.

Make a 'success list'. This is a list of *everything* you are successful at, or have been a success at.

Go back as far as you can, make a fun thing of it. Get a really big piece of paper and keep adding to your list.

You see – you *are* a success!

# CHOOSE THE COLOURS YOU NEED

We all respond to colour and scientists have discovered that each colour sends a unique message to the brain which affect our moods in different ways.

Look at the colours below and think about how your own clothes and decor can enhance particular moods:

- ☆ RED is physically stimulating.

- ☆ YELLOW is good for increasing optimism.

- ☆ ORANGE increases security; wear it to lift your love life.

- ☆ GREEN represents natural healing and balance.

- ☆ Wear PINK to attract some TLC (tender loving care).

- ☆ BLUE is good for when you want to appear cool.

- ☆ PURPLE increases spiritual awareness.

# INCREASE YOUR
# PERSONAL POWER

When we are high in personal power we are:

- *High in self-esteem*
- *Energetic and dynamic*
- *Effective*
- *Imaginative*

*Purposeful*

*Decisive*

*Focused*

How often do you feel like this?
If we want to be high in personal power we
have to take total responsibility for
everything that happens to us in our life.

Take charge of your life: say 'no' when you
need to; express your true feelings and don't
let people treat you like a doormat.

Let go of blame, increase your personal
power and be free to live your life
dynamically.

# SOFTEN YOUR FOCUS

*This world is a wonderful place.*

How do you respond to this statement? We often let our life become humdrum and ordinary.

As the years pass we are inclined to live our lives more and more according to our habits.

Here is a technique to lift you out of your habitual behaviour into a state of alert and enhanced awareness.

- ☆ Become aware of the focus of your vision. How far are you looking?

- ☆ Now stop and expand your awareness, you will feel your focus 'softening' as you do this.

Look for more and you will experience more! Keep practising.

# MAKE YOUR OWN MISSION STATEMENT

What is your mission statement?

In other words, what is your life's purpose, why exactly are you here? To raise consciousness about environmental issues? To make the world a happier place? To ensure that your children have high self-esteem? To make people laugh?

When you can make a mission statement your life will have new direction and purpose.

Remember that you bring your own unique set of skills and strengths to this planet and you came here to use those abilities.

Discover what drives you from within and match it with real-world activities to give your life new meaning.

# HAVE A THINK SLIM, BE SLIM DAY

You know those days when you wake up feeling lethargic, bloated and overfed and low in the attraction stakes?

Get a grip on your day and turn in into a 24-hour programme which will take off a little weight, make you feel spiritually lighter, more in control and will increase your feelings of self-respect.

Keep your diet as light and pure as you can.
Drink hot water with lemon juice every
couple of hours to detoxify your system.

Plan some exercise time and relaxation time
throughout the day.

Tomorrow you will wake up feeling better,
brighter and lighter.

# Enjoy the Music
## of the Spheres

When you feel caught on the treadmill of life, STOP! Try this simple yet wonderful meditation technique.

Relax and close your eyes. Now tune in to any inner sound that you can hear in your head.

Home in on it until it is the main sound in your mind. Let all other sounds and thoughts pass by.

As you let this sound fill your consciousness you will ultimately merge with it until you can no longer hear it.

Listen for as long as you feel comfortable and enjoy what is called 'the music of the spheres'.

# APPRECIATE YOUR TEAM

Do you know who is in your team?

Here I'm not referring to your local football team but to any group of people who work and co-operate with you.

You might belong to any number of teams: your work team, your family, the parent group at school, a darts club, sports club, drama group … there are numerous possibilities. Make a list of all your teams.

Being part of a team increases our sense of belonging and well-being. There is nothing quite like the shared feeling of a team achievement.

Think about your own teams and appreciate your own team members.

# STAY FOREVER YOUNG

We can enjoy the freedom of adulthood and the pleasures of childhood if we remain young at heart.

Fun people can be any age: staying young is an attitude, it has nothing to do with how old we are.

Get in touch with some of the childhood memories which link you to your past.

These may be rekindled by any sense experience: the touch of velvet; the taste of an acid drop; the smell of the sea; the sound of a church bell; a ride on a swing …

Recreate some childhood experiences to stay forever young.

# MAKE GOOD
# VIBRATIONS

You can raise your energetic vibrations and feel lighter by using uplifting words and thoughts when you speak to yourself and to others.

If you feel anxious use positive words to raise your energy.

Say such words to yourself as: HARMONY, LOVE, PEACE, RADIANCE, BEAUTY, JOY, ENTHUSIASM, COMMITTED, DELIGHTFUL, INSPIRED … Think and speak of all the beautiful and inspiring words you know.

Notice how you feel lighter and brighter when you use these words in conversation.

Use uplifting words in the company of others; watch and feel the changes in their energy and yours.

# SEARCH FOR THE HERO INSIDE YOURSELF

Who do you most admire? Who are your own personal heroes and heroines?

Make a list of your heroes and write down exactly why you admire them. Think carefully about the qualities that you most admire in these people. And now think about yourself.

At some level you already have these qualities. If you can recognize certain strengths in others then you must also be aware of the capacity for these same strengths in yourself (otherwise you would never have recognized them).

Search for the hero inside yourself who is able to use these gifts to create a full and incredible life.

# RESPECT
# PARENTHOOD

When the dinner is burning and the washing machine has broken down and you only had three hours sleep last night, remember: you are not alone!

Parents everywhere do a magnificent job, so remind yourself to respect the act of parenthood.

Make a list of the following points and refer to it constantly.

- ✨ Parenthood is a *big* job.
- ✨ I am doing my best.
- ✨ Parenthood is vital.
- ✨ I *don't* have to feel guilty.
- ✨ I need to look after myself.
- ✨ There are no perfect parents.
- ✨ I forgive and thank my mother and father.
- ✨ I *can* let go.

Put this list in a prominent place!

# TAKE YOUR DAY
# ONE STEP AT A TIME

Not every day starts with a bang. Sometimes it's hard to find the energy to get up and out.

You might have a lot on your mind; you may have a busy schedule; there may be difficulties to face.

When your day gets off to a dreary start *take one step at a time.*

Concentrate on the immediate task in hand.

Just get yourself out of bed before you think of the next job. Don't think about the next step until the immediate step is over.

As you achieve more and more tasks you will start to feel in control again.

# DO WHATEVER TURNS YOU ON

It is not necessary to take mood altering drugs in order to change the way that we feel.

Think of how easily your emotions can be changed by the simple things in life.

Perhaps a certain piece of music can lift your spirits, a walk, a piece of artwork, sex, a poem, surfing, driving, cooking, swimming, dancing, shopping, singing … there are an infinite number of possibilities here.

Start to notice what changes your mood for the better.

Make a list of the things that energize and excite you. Now *do* these things!

# LOOK FOR THE
# SILVER LINING

Life is full of ups and downs but we can
learn from everything that happens to us.

A relationship ends; we fail an exam; lose a
job … Once the initial anger/dependency/
depression is over we can review our
setbacks and use them to learn more about
ourselves.

Every event in our lives has a purpose – there is a powerful intention in every situation.

Rather than remaining in a negative state which only pulls you down, approach the situation in a new way.

As one door closes another opens. Look for the newly opening door, look for the silver lining …

# NURTURE YOURSELF
## FOR A DAY

☼ Do you treat yourself in a caring way?

☼ Do you love and encourage yourself?

☼ Do you help yourself up when you fall and comfort yourself when you are sad?

☆ Do you forgive yourself when you make a mistake?

We find it so difficult to treat ourselves in this loving and nurturing way.

Decide to nurture yourself for a day and see how it goes.

Let every thought and action support you and say the following affirmation to yourself:

*I deserve love and care.*

Nurture yourself for a day and the habit may grow.

# STAY COOL

If you are feeling worried, nervous, angry, upset or irritable try 'The Emotion Cooler':

- Put your right thumb over your right nostril, just lightly closing it off.

- Exhale. Inhale slowly through your left nostril only for twenty complete breaths.

☀ Keep you mouth closed all the time.

☀ Make the breaths as long and smooth as you can.

☀ Each time you exhale let go of all tension, hurt, anger, irritability and any other negative emotions.

Visualize these emotions draining out of your body so that you feel clear and positive.

Do this exercise now, before the heat is on, and feel the difference in your relaxation levels.

# UNDERSTAND AND INCREASE YOUR SELF-ESTEEM

*All* human beings struggle with issues of self-esteem – yes even those oh-so-confident-looking folk!

It seems as if our self-esteem is always on the line. We can go up and down and up and down again with alarming speed. (Does this sound like you?)

Our self-esteem is rather like a beautiful but delicate flower that needs constant nourishment and care in order for it to grow and remain protected.

Use the tips in this book and as you cultivate ways to bring positive changes into your life your self-esteem will become more stable.

# DISCOVER YOUR
# LIFE'S PURPOSE

Sit quietly, relax and close your eyes. Imagine that your life's work can be represented by a symbol.

Visualize yourself holding your symbol close to your body and feel its energy filling your whole being. There is a hill ahead of you.

Carry your symbol to the top where you see an arched gateway. This gateway leads to your future.

As you step through, throw your symbol high in the air so that it flies out into the world which is your future.

This powerful visualization will help you to attract your life's purpose.

# JUST DO IT

What is it that you would most love to do
but are afraid to do because of the
consequences?

 Name three things that you would love
to do but that you are afraid to try.

☆ Ask yourself what would be the best and worst possible outcomes of doing each of these three things.

☆ Ask yourself, 'What are my fears and anxieties?' and write them down.

How realistic are your fears? Usually fears are irrational and groundless; our longing by far outweighs the reality of the fear itself.

Go ahead – just do it! You will feel fantastic.

# TREASURE YOUR VALUABLES

What is valuable to you? What do you most treasure in your life?

We're not talking about gold watches and diamonds here but rather things that you feel that you cannot do without.

What is important to you in your emotional life? What feelings and people are important? What inspires you, makes you feel good, energizes you?

Your valuables are whatever makes you 'come alive'. Make a list of them. Think about why you value these things – why are they so precious to you?

Take time to appreciate and treasure your valuables.

# EXPECT A MIRACLE

Miracles are love in action. If you don't believe in them they will never happen to you.

We can attract miracles into our lives but only if we truly believe they are possible.

Forget about not *really* allowing yourself to believe in case you are disappointed.

Fear of disappointment will stand in your way forever! Expect a miracle for a week.

Wholeheartedly believe that one will happen and keep trusting. The miracle might not be the one you were expecting but I can assure you that something amazing will happen.

Belief is the most powerful magic of all.

# LOVE YOUR ENEMIES

Someone once described the act of hating and resenting as being like 'hugging a poisonous snake to our bosom'.

Feelings of ill-will fester and eventually erupt, often making us ill.

Make a list of all those people who you can't stand. When you next meet a person on your list imagine that it is their last day on earth and that you will never see them again.

Take this chance to change the nature of your relationship. Forgiveness is hard but possible and will make you feel *fantastic*.

The gifts it brings are the greatest we can receive.

# HEAL YOUR LIFE

However ill you feel, whatever psychological problems you face, you can still be in control of your own healing.

If you have a physical condition find out all you can about it – don't expect the doctor to 'sort you out'. Take the prescribed medicine but also investigate alternative approaches.

Look at your lifestyle and nutrition:

☆ Do they support good health?

☆ Are your relationships supportive or stressful?

☆ Do you love your work or is it winding you up?

Look beyond a single symptom; look at the *whole* picture of your life and take charge of your own healing.

# Just Face the
# Music and Dance

'Just face the music and dance' is such a
wonderful phrase.

It conjures up the image of risk-taking,
decision-making, accepting challenges and
making things happen in a harmonious way.

Maybe you will have to learn to say 'no' more often; you might have to put up with some people not liking you or being envious of you, but always remember, *whose life is this anyway?* Decide to be assertive.

Face the challenges that life brings in a positive way and dance to your own tune.

Dance and the world will dance with you.

# CALM YOUR MIND

Sit comfortably, close your eyes and turn your attention to your breathing.

Notice the muscle in your abdomen, just below your rib cage, which rises and falls as you breathe. Follow its movement.

Each time the muscle rises think, 'Rising' and every time it falls, think 'Falling'. Rising … falling … rising … falling … Let all your other thoughts drift away as you focus on this muscle.

At first your mind will keep wandering off. Each time it does follow it and bring it back to focus on 'Rising … falling … rising …'

Keep trying for a few minutes each day – it gets easier.

# SEND YOUR INNER CRITIC ON HOLIDAY

Deep down we are all excessively self-critical.

Even the most seemingly confident people have a well-developed 'Inner Critic'. The Inner Critic is that part of each of us which nags away and is *never* satisfied with our performance.

You can easily recognize its voice: it's the one which tells you off all the time; the one that keeps saying that you are never good enough /clever enough/thin enough/educated enough ... to do or be anything of note in this world. Learn to recognize this voice and ignore its nagging.

Love and value yourself instead.

# CREATE YOUR OWN
# HEALTH FARM

Allow yourself a whole day to enjoy a health farm extravaganza in the privacy of your own home.

Planning is important so decide beforehand exactly how you will spend your day.

# PLANNING YOUR DAY

- ☼ Buy any beauty items or toiletries that you might need.

- ☼ Choose some beautiful relaxing music and some aromatherapy oils to burn.

- ☼ Shop for some delicious nutritional food. Buy some pure fruit juice and spring water to drink throughout the day.

Start your day by unplugging the phone and switching off TVs and computers.

When you spend a day just pampering yourself you will feel refreshed and invigorated.

# CARPE DIEM –
# SEIZE THE DAY

If you were told that you had four weeks to
live, what would you do immediately?

What would you want to say to whom?

Make a list of all the important things that
you would feel you had to do:

-☆- ...............................................-

-☆- ...............................................-

-☆- ...............................................-

We are not immortal although we often live our lives as if we were. Take a look at the world as if you only had four weeks left – it seems different, doesn't it? *Seize the day*, today.

Do what you know really needs doing.

Live it dynamically, give it all you've got and just see what it gives you back.

# BE HAPPY
## TO DO IT

We all know that the words we use affect the way that we feel.

If we speak negatively we attract negativity and feel negative, and the opposite is also true.

Sometimes we use very small, seemingly innocuous words which can dramatically affect the quality of our lives.

When we say we have 'got to' do something we put ourselves under pressure.

Just notice how you're feeling when you next use that phrase. Watch your words: replace 'I've got to' with 'I'll be happy to' and you might even stop having headaches.

I guarantee that it will make you laugh.

# NEVER *EVER* GIVE UP

When your life is hard and difficulties seem to appear whichever way you turn it is natural to feel dejected.

When we are within the midst of a trauma we will not be inclined to take helpful advice on how to 'feel better'.

We need to experience the sadness, grief, anger, rage, hurt, shame or whatever other strong emotions we are going through.

However, the darkest light is truly just before the dawn. Never *ever* give up on the miraculous process of life.

Believe in yourself and know that you can and will feel hopeful and joyous again.

**Lynda Field** is a trained counsellor and psychotherapist specializing in personal and group development.

Her other books include the best-selling

*Creating Self-Esteem,*
*The Self-Esteem Workbook,*
*Self-Esteem for Women*
and *60 Tips for Self-Esteem.*

She lives in Essex, England.